Embedded Graphics Processing Units

by Patrick H. Stakem

(c) 2017

Number 18 in the Computer
Architecture Series

Table of Contents

Introduction

This book covers the topic of the technology and applications of Embedded Graphics Processing Units. We first discuss what a graphics processing unit is, and how they have taken over the high performance computing market. We take a look at massively parallel microprocessor-based systems, an evolution from parallel mainframes, and see how this is applied to GPU's. Then, we take a look at embedded processors, derived from CPU's. We can then see how all of this practice was rapidly applied to GPU's.

A major topic is the software to program and debug these unit, which are capable of Tera-mistakes per second. We will explore some of the commercial products, and applications. Fasten your seat belt – it's that kind of a technology.

Multicore techniques are now being applied to embedded processors as well. This enables some techniques that were not previously available. In the embedded world, the cores do not necessarily need to be the same. Actually, this technique was used for the Intel floating point co-processor, the 80387, was incorporated onto the same chip as the integer processor, the 80386, in the design of the follow-on 80486 chip. Today, multiple integer cores can share the same silicon substrate with specialized floating point, digital signal and vector processing, and specialized media and video engines. The individual cores can implement superscalar, super-pipelined, or other optimization techniques. Essentially, we have MIMD (multiple instruction, multiple data) parallel processing chip for embedded applications. Nothing is ever free, though. The challenge, as always, will be the programming.

That's being addressed with new tool-kits tying into to standard libraries. The Cloud was nice while it lasted, but there are issues with transmission of data, and security. Now, you hold the cloud in your hand, hidden in the more-and-more capable phone.

Author

The author has a BSEE in Electrical Engineering from Carnegie-Mellon University, and Masters Degrees in Applied Physics and Computer Science from the Johns Hopkins University. During a career as a NASA support contractor from 1971 to 2013, he worked at all of the NASA Centers. He served as a mentor for the NASA/GSFC Summer Robotics Engineering Boot Camp at GSFC for 2 years. He taught Embedded Systems for the Johns Hopkins University, Engineering for Professionals Program, for the Graduate Computer Science Program for Loyola University in Maryland, and for Capital Institute of Technology. He has done several summer Cubesat Programs at the undergraduate and graduate level.

Mr. Stakem can be found on LinkedIn. Comments, corrections, suggestions are appreciated.

The Architectures

This sections discusses the various computer architectures that lead to the development of the gpu, and the evolution processors take from desktop/server to embedded.

The ALU

The arithmetic logic unit performs arithmetic and logic functions on binary integer data, and provides flow of control. The arithmetic functions we would like to have performed are additional, subtraction, multiplication, and division.

The *Von Neuman Architecture* says there is no distinction between the code and the data. This was an observation by John von Neumann of the Institute for Advanced Studies at Princeton University. While consulting for the Moore School of Electrical Engineering at the University of Pennsylvania, von Neumann wrote an incomplete "First Draft of a Report on the EDVAC" (computer). The paper described a computer architecture in which the data and the program are both stored in the computer's memory in the same address space. Before this, it was the custom to have separate code and data storage (the Harvard architecture), and they were not necessarily the same size or format. Von Neumann observed that the code is also data. Most modern microprocessors are this style. For speed, especially in digital signal processors, designers revert to the older *Harvard* architecture, with separate code and data stores, as this gives a speed-up in accessing from memory.

The FPU

The floating point unit operates on numbers in the floating point format. As ALU's operate on integers, FPU's operate on numbers in the engineering/scientific notation, with a mantissa, and an exponent. These are, themselves, binary integers. Originally, floating point operations were done in custom software packages. This was very slow, but better than nothing. Then, floating point units were developed, that operated on the mantissa and the exponent separately. The early units did not fetch their own data or instructions, but relied on the CPU to do that for them. This was a very simple case of parallelism; the ALU could be operating on integer data while the FPU was operating on floating point formatted data. As technology progressed, the FPU hardware was absorbed into the ALU chip. It is important to remember that the FPU does not concern itself with logical operations (AND, OR, Negate). These are done in the ALU. Now, the FPU and ALU are a linked pair. In addition, with multicore, multiples of each pair can occupy the same silicon.

The GPU

The GPU is optimized for video data processing. It is very fast, but not as versatile as an CPU. It operates on its own data formats. It is optimized to be amazingly fast at what it does. Following the same path, multi-core GPU's can be built. In fact, these are now the basis for most of the World's supercomputers.

We have the technology to combine a CPU, FPU, and GPU on a chip, in fact, multiple copies of each. This is called multicore. What will make or break the architecture is fast interconnection among the units. Approaches for this were developed for massively parallel multiprocessors, where each node was a box, or a board. Now the nodes have shrunk to a chip. The interconnect architecture can remain the same.

The graphics processing unit performs specific arithmetic operations on image data. These were introduced in the late 1990's as specialized architectures optimized for processing of large blocks of graphics data in parallel. Their instruction set is targeted to operations performed on 3D graphics data, such as transformations and rendering. Although these were originally targeted to computer gaming applications, it was not lost on scientists and engineers that this was the type of matrix manipulation and digital filtering that they employed in many different areas. The GPU is not general-purpose, but is targeted and optimized to operate on matrix data structures. GPU's are now used for many general-purpose scientific and engineering computing across a range of platforms. The term GPU was invented by high-performance graphics vendor nVidia.

GPU computing is possible because today's GPU does a lot more than just render graphics: It might achieve a teraflop of floating point performance.

The first GPU's were designed as graphics accelerators, supporting only specific fixed-function pipelines. Starting in the late 1990s, the hardware became increasingly programmable. Less than a year after the GPU first appeared, it was being applied in various technical computing fields because of its excellent floating point performance. The General Purpose GPU, GPGPU as nVidia calls it, had appeared. Derived from that, we get GPU computing.

Initially, GPU's ran graphics programming languages such as OpenGL. Developers had to map scientific calculations onto problems that could be represented by triangles and polygons. A breakthrough came when a group of Stanford University researchers set out to re-purpose the GPU as a "streaming processor."

In 2003, *Brook* was introduced as the first widely adopted programming model to extend C with data-parallel constructs. Using concepts such as streams, kernels and reduction operators, the Brook compiler and runtime system presented the GPU as a general-purpose processor in a high-level language. Most importantly, Brook programs were not only easier to write than hand-tuned GPU code, they were many times faster. GPU's process high speed video data on phones, tablets, and tv's, and also find wide application in scientific and financial computing.

Massively parallel computers started out as large numbers of commodity computer boards, linked with a high speed interconnect. This evolved into commodity

9

off-the-shelf microprocessors, using the same interconnects. The same technique is applicable to commodity GPU products. GPU's, as we cautioned, are not general purpose processors. However, they can address a large range of computationally intensive tasks if you format the data they way they expect it. They can cooperate with each other, if the necessary communication infrastructure is available. All this relies on the available of good software tools, and development environments.

The first processor to include a graphics unit was the Texas Instruments' TMS-34010 in 1986. Before this, a GPU was a separate chip. Now, the functionality has been included along with the cpu. GPU's can be included with the cpu, or be a standalone unit.

A GPU is a specialized computer architecture to manipulate image data at high rates. The GPU devices are highly parallel, and specifically designed to handle image data, and operations on that data. They do this much fastest than a programmed general purpose CPU. Most desktop machines have the GPU function on a video card or integrated with their CPU. Originally, GPU's were circuit card based. Now, they're chips, and increasingly, multi-core chips. GPU operations are very memory intensive. The GPU design is customized to SIMD type operations.

The instruction set of the GPU is specific to graphics operations on block data. The requirements were driven by the demands of 2-D and 3-D video games on pc's, phones, tablets, and dedicated gaming units. As GPU units became faster and more capable, they began to consume more power (and thus generate more heat) than the associated CPU's. The GPU operations are typically memory intensive, so fast access to memory is critical.

A GPU is generally a dataflow architecture, as opposed to a control-flow, Von Neumann machine. The instructions executed depend on the inputs, to the extent that the order of execution is non-deterministic. On general purpose machines implementing graphics processing code, the behavior would be deterministic.

Although designed to process video data, some GPU's have been used as adjunct data processors and accelerators in other areas involving vectors and matrices, such as the inverse discrete cosine transform. Types of higher-level processing implemented by GPU's include texture mapping, polygon rendering, object rotation, and coordination system transformation. They also support object shading operations, data oversampling, and interpolation. GPU's find a major application area in video decoding. Building on this, GPU's enable advanced features in digital cameras such as facial recognition, or eye tracking. GPU's can be used to accelerate database operations such as gather and scatter, vertex operations. A vertex is where lines (or vectors) meet. GPU's have enabled the optical-sensed lane departure feature on cars, and are helping to enable self-driving cars.

GPU's can tackle the embarrassingly parallel problems in engineering and physics, those that map to multiple parallel tasks that can be executed simultaneously. Examples of some of these applications include protein folding and ray tracing. Practical, affordable systems are being built with hundred's of thousands of interconnected GPU's.

You can do general purpose computing on a GPU, although it may not be the ideal platform. It requires you to recast your computation in a way the GPU understands, which is to say, in terms of graphics. So, we might have to represent the data as a 2D or 3D object, that we can apply the GPU's operations on. GPU's are special purpose devices that have instruction sets that are not general purpose, and are intended specifically for graphics data processing, and problems that lend themselves to stream or vector processing. GPU's are stream processors, in that they operate in parallel on multiple data. Given the right problem, that is map-able into the GPU's architecture, a huge performance gain of orders of magnitude can be achieved, over regular CPU's.

One figure of merit in GPU's is their arithmetic intensity, defined as the number of operations per memory access. You might think of this as a computation:communication ratio.

GPU's are used for coordinate system transformations, and for science data processing. The GPU can implement such operations as shading, codec, mapping, video decoding, and 3D image manipulation. A big driver for the development and enhancement of GPU's is video games, digital cameras, and tv's.

Extensive code libraries exist for GPU's, and different problem domains, from physics modeling, to video gaming and virtual reality. API's include OpenGL and Directx. OpenGL, the Open (source) graphics libraries operate across languages and platforms. It was introduced in 1992. It is an industry standard, and claims scalability from hand-held to supercomputer. It consists of a series of library functions, callable from most computer languages. DirectX, similarly, has a set of runtime libraries. It is a Microsoft product. There are other libraries of graphics functions available as well.

GPU's need high bandwidth connections to data. They are beginning to include fast, hardware managed, multi--level caches. The architectures differ from that of general purpose caches, since the GPU is mostly accessing vector data, from consecutive memory locations. GPU's have large register files on chip to reduce access time to frequently used data.

Graphics Data Structure

Graphics data can be integer or floating point. Generally, it is organized in one dimensional arrays (vectors) or multi-dimensional arrays. Since we will see later that we can under use our GPU to do general purpose processing, there is nothing special about the data format. Keep in mind, the GPU does not implement logic functions.

To use the GPU in this way, we basically have to reformulate our computational problem in terms of the graphics operations the GPU provides. The OpenCL language, widely used in GPU programming, is general purpose.

Graphic Operations on data

Besides the usual add, subtract, multiply, and divide, there are some unique operations for graphics data. This include min, max, average, among others. We could accomplish these with a quick couple of lines of code, but it is much faster, once we develop an opcode to do it. Also, in graphics processing, it is common to have multiple units working on multiple data with the same operation at the same time.

Actually, before we discuss operations in the GPU, let's take a look at Single-instruction, Multiple data (SIMD, one technique in parallel computing.

If one computer is fast, a bunch of them is faster, right? Yes, if we do it correctly. Massively parallel computers started out as large numbers of commodity computer boards, linked with a high speed interconnect. This evolved into commodity off-the-shelf microprocessors, using the same interconnects. The same technique is applicable to commodity GPU products. GPU's, as we cautioned, are not general purpose processors. However, they can address a large range of computationally intensive tasks if you format the data they way they expect it. They can cooperate with each other, if the necessary communication infrastructure is available. All this relies on the available of good software tools, and development environments.

The bottleneck to getting more than one processor to work on a given problem domain at one time is the communications. There is an upper bound in a bus-oriented, shared memory Symmetric Multiprocessing (SMP) systems, arising from the communication limit of the bus interconnect (a classic Shannon channel limit). Clusters of computers also suffer from an inter-processor communication limit, from the LAN-like interconnect. We can use a message passing approach, or shared memory for inter-processor communication. And keep in mind, each node of the architecture can be more than a single processor – we can have a mesh of meshes in a hierarchical fashion.

Another technique is to put multiple cpu/gpu units on a single chip, and use that as a node in a compute network. This is called Multicore technology. Multicore computer architecture uses two or more (up to 100's and 1,000's) of cpu's, configured into a multiprocessor on a single chip. Each cpu can fetch and execute its own instructions, and has a method to communicate with the other cpu's. If an embedded chip has a cpu, memory, and I/O on a single chip, a multicore architecture has an entire network of parallel processors on a single chip. In the same sense that a computer used to fill a room, then was reduced to a box, then to a chip, we now see a further reduction of multiple cpu's. It's just Moore's law. Every 18 months or so, the technology can give us a 2x factor of improvement. So far, so good.

For the longest time, the state of the technology only allowed putting one cpu on a chip. As things progressed along the lines of Moore's Law, the separate floating point unit was incorporated onto the same chip. Then came cache memory. We are now at the point where we can put multiple cpu's on a chip; these being called cores. But just being able to cram more cpu's on a single piece of silicon doesn't solve our high-performance problem. There are bottlenecks introduced in this approach, and they must be addressed. This lesson was learned many years ago with multiprocessors. The technology has changed, but the architectural limitations are the same.

The limitations to computer performance tend to be either the instruction rate of the cpu itself, or the channel capacity of the various data paths involved. One approach to increased performance is parallelism.

Some performance enhancements come from the architecture of the multiprocessor. For example, interrupt processing can be offloaded to a non-busy cpu.

One issue is how interrupts are handled in multiprocessing. How are interrupts steered to the proper processor? It is a function of the operating system. In the same way that processes are assigned to certain processors, interrupts and their associated interrupt handling are also assigned. Binding interrupts to specific cpu's is not necessarily the proper approach; since this approach does not improve hits in cache memory Multiple interrupts can overload the selected processor. Handling interrupts is a task, and task allocation is a function of the operating system. A multiprocessing operating system is required to manage the unique issues of multiprocessor hardware.

Another issue is cache coherency. In multicore architectures, each CPU core has its own L1 cache, but shares L2 caches with other cores. Local data in the L1 caches must be consistent with data in other L1 caches. If one core changes a value in cache due to a write operation, that data needs to be changed in all other caches as well.

A multi-core processor has multiple cpu and memory elements in a single chip. Being on a single chip reduces the communications times between elements, and allows for multiprocessing. Advances in microelectronics fabrication techniques lead to the implementation of multicores for desktop and server machines around 2007. It was becoming increasingly difficult to increase clock speeds, so the obvious approach was to turn to parallelism. Currently, in this market, quad-core, 6-core, 8-core, and higher chips are available. Besides additional cpu's, additional on-chip memory must be added, usually in the form of memory caches, to keep the processors fed with instructions and data. There is no inherent difference in multicore architectures and multiprocessing with single core chips, except in the speed of communications. The standard interconnect techniques used in multiprocessing and clustering are applied to inter-core communications.

Coupling between cores can be tight or loose. A tightly coupled system usually is implemented with shared memory. A loosely coupled system generally uses communication channels between cores.

Massively Parallel Architectures

This section will discuss the architectural approaches in using large numbers of microprocessors connected together into one machine. Single chip Massively Parallel Microprocessor Systems (MPMS) nodes need an interconnect methodology. Later, multiple compute chips on a single substrate require a fast on-chip interconnect.

In this section, we address architectural approaches to coordinating the use of multiple processors. Most of these approaches will work with any underlying technology, and are useful after the maximum speed of a single processor in a given technology has been wrung out.

Shared memory MPP's usually do not have a homogeneous communication environment, due to communication bandwidth restrictions. A two-tier communications architecture is used, with shared memory intrabox, and a lan type point-point link for interbox messaging. Since MPP machines have to scale to thousands of processors, a distributed memory scheme is usually chosen. Another approach is to cluster SMP's. Data sharing is the key, and the critical issue for large parallel relational database applications. The performance will be made (or broken) by the sophistication of the interconnection scheme. Speed and latency are of critical importance. Latency predominates for short messages.

Consider the case of having to send a large volume of data from New York to California. We look at two options: we rent a gigabit-class line, and transfer the data serially at OC-48, or about 2.4 gigabits per second. The latency, from the time a bit enters the line at New York until it exits at California, is very short, and depends on the time it takes light to traverse 2000 miles of cable. This is an expensive option. We could also decide to charter a 747 freighter, and load it with flash drives. Here, the latency is about 5 hours, but the data all arrives together. One case emphasizes speed, the other case emphasizes low latency.

Again, let's look at an analogy. If we want to get across town using the bus system, we wait at the bus stop for the next available bus. The wait time is our latency, and is random, depending on when we arrive with respect to the bus's arrival. If we go only a few blocks, the latency may be commensurate with or even exceed the travel time. If we go across country on the bus, the latency is totally dominated by the travel time. Even in town, if we need to change buses, we introduce another latency between getting dropped off by bus-1 and picked up by bus-2. We may need to cross town in several of these 'hops', each with its own latency. For one person, this may not be efficient. For large aggregates of people, it makes sense.

Alternately, we can call an Uber, and go directly from where we are to our destination. There is still a wait-latency, but the travel time is reduced, and the cost is higher.

In the interconnect hierarchy, the node-node connection is frequently made via shared memory. Thus, a node may be an Symmetrical Multi-Processor (SMP) architecture in its own right, with two or four processor elements. this approach does not scale well beyond about 16 processors. The node-node communication is tightly coupled.

Between nodes, a loosely coupled message passing scheme is usually employed. This uses a LAN-like architecture that can take one of many topological forms. Popular are the mesh, torus, hypercube, and tree.

Supercomputer on a Module

Rather than a big box of interconnected boards, we can now have a single circuit card with multiple computer nodes, and, more recently, multiple computer units on a single chip. These compute units can be ALU's, FPU's, or GPU's. The interconnect between units really doesn't affect how the data is processed. GPU's can access their data differently in memory, and that can affect the memory architecture. One instance of this came from Intel in 2015. It is a pci-E add-in card, with a 72-core Knight's Landing chip, and 16G of ram. It can achieve 8 teraflops. Compare that to the first generation Cray-1 supercomputer, at 160 megaflops. The Intel module is 50,000 times faster.

Intel is a player in the Supercomputer world, with units based on its Xeon and Xenon-Phi X-86-64 architectures, with the (Advanced Vector Extensions) AVX-512 extensions. The Phi 7250, has 68 cores, supported with 34 megabytes of L2 cache. Cores operate at 1.4 GHz, with a turbo burst frequency of 1.6. These chips dissipate in excess of 200 watts. The Phi series does not currently support virtualization. They can support a total of 284 gigabytes of memory, on 6 channels. These cpu's are the backbone of Intel's Scalable System Framework (SSF).

Intel is currently in its 10th generation of GPU's. The first-gen unit, the Intel 740 dates to 1998, and was supported by OpenGL. By the fifth generation, in 2010, each execution engine had a 128 bit wide floating point unit, that executed four 32-bit operations per clock. By the eighth generation, each EU had dual SIMD-4 FPU's, with clock rates just below a gigahertz.

The Intel Xeon Phi is a many-core X86 architecture. The x86 part allows it to run software developed for that architecture, and that core is linked to the GPU core. In 2013, the world's faster supercomputer, the Iianhe-2 in China, was based on 48,000 Xeon-Pi's.

The Intel Knight's Landing is a second generation many-integrated core architecture, circa 2013. It contains up to 72 Atom cores, each core being 4-way multi-threaded. It supports dual AVX-512, 512-bit vector SIMD processors. Knight's Hill is the 3rd generation device. It was focused to deep learning, but was canceled in 2017. The Knight's Mill was the replacement product, coming out in December of 2017. It supports 4-way hyperthreading.

Intel implements Imagination Technologies PowerVR architecture under license. This architecture supports very high speed 3D rendering. Now in their 8th generation, some of the family members are achieving 25 gflops, with an architecture built for Apple capable of 360 Gflops.

Intel has a research program named "Tera-Scale," which targets teraflops of performance. Two prototypes have been built. The first chip, code named Polaris, had 80 cores, and is clocked at more than 3 Ghz. It achieved 1.28 Tflops. Another project, circa 2009, is the single-chip cloud computer with 48 cores arranged in a 6x4, 2-D mesh. Intel is moving away from the iconic x86 architecture to a VLIW approach. Cores can be put to sleep when not needed, to conserve power. An approach called die-stacking is used, where CPU, flash, and DRAM die are stacked, reducing memory bus latencies.

Embedded Processors

The embedded computer can be characterized by the parameters of its central processing unit (CPU), memory, and input/output (I/O). The CPU parameters of importance are speed, power consumption, word size, and price. The memory parameters include power consumption, volatility, and size or capacity. I/O characteristics must be matched to external systems components.

Most microprocessors sold, by volume, are destined for embedded applications as opposed to desktop or server use. Embedded systems have limited or no human intervention. They are purpose-built, and self-contained. Many include the features of BIST – built-in self-test.

Embedded systems can be found in most consumer products. Embedded systems, as opposed to traditional general-purpose desktop computers or tablets, are targeted toward a specific application or market, have specialized I/O, and limited user interfaces.

Embedded systems are generally dedicated to a single task or small set of related tasks; have limited human interface; have special purpose interfaces; and are mostly self-contained.

Many embedded systems are required to be real-time - they have strict deadlines. Others are event-driven - a trigger event kicks off a predetermined sequence of responses. Embedded systems are almost always resource constrained. The resources might be size, weight, power, throughput, heat generation, reliability, deadlines, etc. Embedded systems have a high non-recurring engineering (NRE) cost (development cost), but are generally cheap to produce in volume. Embedded computers do not usually host their own development system. These are generally hosted on a pc.

Embedded processors, until a while back, consisted of a CPU, Memory, and I/O. The next set, as the technology evolved, was multiple CPU's, more memory, and better I/O. Then GPU's cam along, and were built into embedded computers. These were mostly board level products, targeting computer graphics. We are are at this writing is multi-core GPU's, integrated with memory and I/O.

Along the way, GPU's were shown to out-compute CPU's, and now, mostly every Supercomputer on the planet is based on a Massively Parallel Architecture of GPU's. The trick is to make that technology 1) cheaper, and 2) mobile.

A CPU, you recall, executes logical, math, and control instructions from memory. It works with integers. An FPU does math operations on the Floating Point data format, and some control instructions. Usually a CPU includes a companion FPU on chip, both sharing the same memory. A GPU is a specialty ALU that operated on graphics (video) data structures, with a reduced instruction set tailored to that type of data.

Originally, RISC was a concept to speed up processing. The instruction set was purged of all the "hard" instructions such as divide. The idea was, only include instructions that could execute in one clock cycle. That makes pipelining easier. More time-consuming instructions, such as divide, are also less frequently used, and can be handled in a type of microcode.

The GPU sets out with an integer instruction set, and usually has an FPU. The instructions are tailored to integers, and special formats used in representing image data.

MultiCore means we have more than one compute core on a chip. We can have multiple ALU's and FPU's, with a communications structure to handle the data. These are essentially parallel processors on a chip. It's gotten to the point where we can put a lot of these on a chip, so we have a chip-level massively parallel processor. What used to take a room, now takes a chip. We can do the same thing with GPU's.

The problem with GPU's is, they are not really general purpose. Their instruction set is tied to, predominately. video data streams. They can handle normal integers.

A GPU is a specialized computer architecture to manipulate image data at high rates. It can be a single chip, or incorporated with a general purpose CPU. The GPU devices are highly parallel, and specifically designed to handle image data, and operations on that data. They do this much fastest than a programmed general purpose CPU. Most desktop machines have the GPU function on a video card or integrated with their CPU. Originally, GPU's were circuit card based. GPU operations are very memory intensive. The GPU design is customized to SIMD type operations.

The instruction set of the GPU is specific to graphics operations on block data. The requirements were driven by the demands of 2-D and 3-D video games on pc's, phones, tablets, and dedicated gaming units. As GPU units became faster and more capable, they began to consume more power (and thus generate more heat) than the associated CPU's.

Although designed to process video data, some GPU's have been used as adjunct data processors and accelerators in other areas involving vectors and matrices, such as the inverse discrete cosine transform. Types of higher-level processing implemented by GPU's include texture mapping, polygon rendering, object rotation, and coordination system transformation. They also support object shading operations, data oversampling, and interpolation. GPU's find a major application area in video decoding. Building on this, GPU's enable advanced features in digital cameras such as facial recognition, or eye tracking.

In multicore architectures, each CPU core may have its own L1 cache, but share L2 caches with other cores. Local data in the L1 caches must be consistent with data in other L1 caches. If one core changes a value in cache due to a write operation, that data needs to be changed in other caches as well (if they hold the same item).

This problem is well known from the field of multiprocessing. The issues can be addressed by several mechanisms. In cache snooping, each cache monitors the others for changes. If a change in value is seen, the local cached copy is invalidated. This means it will have to be re-accessed from the next level before use. A global directory of cached data can also be maintained. Protocols for cache coherency include MSI, MESI, and others.

A *multicore processor* has multiple cpu and memory elements in a single chip. Being on a single chip reduces the communications times between elements, and allows for multiprocessing. Advances in microelectronics fabrication techniques lead to the implementation of multicores for desktop and server machines around 2007. It was becoming increasingly difficult to increase clock speeds, so the obvious approach was to turn to parallelism. Currently, in this market, quad-core, 6-core, and 8-core chips are available. Besides additional cpu's, additional on-chip memory must be added, usually in the form of memory caches, to keep the processors fed with instructions and data. There is no inherent difference in multicore architectures and multiprocessing with single core chips, except in the speed of communications. The standard interconnect technologies are applied to inter-core communications.

We can compare multicore devices to large parallel machines of some 10 years past, in the same sense that we can compare a single-chip cpu to large mainframe systems of 20-25 years ago. The architecture is similar, but the implementation is different due to changing technologies.

CUDA

Cuda (Compute Unified Device Architecture) is the dominant proprietary GPU product from Nvidia. To go along with the hardware, nVidia provided massively parallel CDA-c, OpenCL, and DirectCompute software tools. These support not only parallelization, but also debugging of parallel code. GPU-targeted code can be developed by the same process and with the same look-and-feel tools as CPU code. Nvidia's Nexus development environment supports Microsoft Visual Studio, and C++. MATLAB provides a Parallel Computing Toolbox. Nvidia pioneered the use of GPU accelerators in 2007. They come with a set of optimized libraries, and parallelization tools.

Cuda is a parallel computing platform and a programming model. It enables dramatic increases in computing performance by harnessing the power of the graphics processing unit. A CUDA program includes parallel functions (kernels) across parallel threads. The compiler organizes these threads into blocks and grids. A block is a set of concurrently executing threads that can synchronize and co-ordinate. A grid is an array of blocks. In the CUDA programming model a thread has private memory. Each block has shared memory space, as do Grids.

Threads map to processors. Each Gpu unit executes one or more grids. Each streaming multiprocessor executes one or more thread blocks, and CUDA cores, and possibly other execution engines, execute threads.

CUDA introduced a variation on the digital signal processing Multiply-Accumulate operation (AxB+C), called Fused Multiply-ADD (FMA). In traditional Multiply-Add the AxB product will be truncated, but in the FMA, all bits of the produce are retained for the ADD operation.

The implementation of floating point on CUDA is mostly but not completely IEEE compliant. This approach varies with vendor. Most GPU's at this time do not fully support 64-bit floating point data and operations.

Applying the horsepower of the GPU to real problems, the CUDA allows applications to be written in c, c++, Python, and FORTRAN. NVIDIA unveiled CUDA in 2006 as a solution for general-computing on GPU's.

The G-80 chip, introduced in 2006, established the GPU

computing model. It supported the c programming language, and was threaded. It implemented the Single Instruction, Multiple Thread (SIMT) concept. It had a complexity of 680 million-1.4 billion transistors. It did not include L1 or L2 cache.

GPU computing

The focus on large parallel machines has changed from clusters of general purpose ALU's to GPU's. This has taken over the field of high performance computing.

The graphics processing unit performs arithmetic operations on image data. These were introduced in the late 1990's as specialized architectures optimized for processing of large blocks of graphics data in parallel. Their instruction set is targeted to operations performed on 3D graphics data, such as transformations and rendering. Although these were originally targeted to computer gaming applications, it was not lost on scientists and engineers that this was the type of matrix manipulation and digital filtering that they employed in many different areas. The GPU is not general-purpose, but is targeted and optimized to operate on matrix data structures. GPU's are now used for many general-purpose scientific and engineering computing across a range of platforms. The term GPU was invented by high-performance graphics vendor nVidia.

Using high-level languages, GPU-accelerated applications can run the sequential part of the workload on a CPU, optimized for single-threaded performance, while running parallel processing on the GPU. This is called referred to as "GPU computing."

GPU computing is possible because today's GPU does a lot more than just render graphics: It might achieve a teraflop of floating point performance.

The first GPU's were designed as graphics accelerators, supporting only specific fixed-function pipelines. Starting in the late 1990s, the hardware became increasingly programmable. Less than a year after the GPU first appeared, it was being applied in various technical computing fields because of its excellent floating point performance. The General Purpose GPU, GPGPU as nVidia calls it, had appeared. Derived from that, we get GPU-accelerated computing.

Initially, GPU's ran graphics programming languages such as OpenGL. Developers had to map scientific calculations onto problems that could be represented by triangles and polygons. A breakthrough came when a group of Stanford University researchers set out to re-purpose the GPU as a "streaming processor." What's in a name?

In 2003, *Brook* was introduced as the first widely adopted programming model to extend C with data-parallel constructs. Using concepts such as streams, kernels, and reduction operators, the Brook compiler and runtime system presented the GPU as a general-purpose processor in a high-level language. Most importantly, Brook programs were not only easier to write than hand-tuned GPU code, they were many times faster. GPU's process high speed video data on phones, tablets, and tv's, and also find wide application in scientific and financial computing. GPU-based supercomputers are tackling the hard problems, such as SETI- the search for extra-terrestrial intelligence, protein folding, weather forecasting, financial modeling and analysis, and oil and gas exploration.

GPU-based Supercomputers

To give you an idea how mainstream this topic is, just go shopping for "gpu supercomputer" on Google. You'll be amazed how affordable they are. Nvidia has a page on building your own personal supercomputer, based on the Tesla.
(www.nvidia.com/object/tesla_build_your_own.html).
Motherboard manufacturer Asus offers a supercomputing workstation with 7 PCIe slots on the motherboard for the Tesla boards. The heat-pipe based cooling system, and the power supply are well matched to the compute architecture. The motherboard supports an Intel Xenon processor, and triple channel DDR-3 memory.

The Register (www.theregister.co.uk) reported in September of 2015 on "Nine of the world's fastest GPU supercomputers." They mention that of the Top 500 list of supercomputers, 52 used the nVidia GPU.

Let's look at number one (in 2015), the Oak Ridge National Lab's *Titan,* a Cray XL7. It achieved over 17

Petaflops per second, using 262,632 NVIDIA K20x GPU's. It consumes a mere 8.2 Megawatts of power (well, there is a downside). Although, it is one of the most energy efficient machines in the area of Gigaflops per watt, coming in at 2.1. It will be replaced by a faster machine in 2018. A similar Cray XC30 at the Swiss National Super-computing Centre uses 73,808 of the GPU's to achieve 6.2 Petaflops. A commercial system in Australia is a used for stock trading. It is a SGU ICE-X/Superblade, with more than 265,000 cores, achieving 3.5 Petaflops.

Intel is a player in the Supercomputer world, with units based on its Xeon and Xenon-Phi X-86-64 architectures, with the AVX-512 extensions. The Phi 7250, has 68 cores, supported with 34 megabytes of L2 cache. Each operates at 1.4 GHz, with a turbo burst frequency of 1.6. These chips dissipate in excess of 200 watts. The Phi series does not currently support virtualization. They can support a total of 284 gigabytes of memory, on 6 channels. These cpu's are the backbone of Intel's Scalable System Framework (SSF).

The Phi many-core processor are targeted directly to Supercomputers. It is an X-86 architecture. They can be used as stand-alone chips.

Massively Parallel Systems

Massively parallel systems have hundreds or thousands

of cpu's, cooperating on the same problem. The cpu's could be pc's, they could be chips, and now they can be multicore chips.

There are limits to the improvement of program performance in adding more processors. Certainly, we can't have hundreds of people working on this book, with a goal of finishing it in a day. There's too much coordination required. It has been observed that the serial portion of the program, the part that can't be parallelized, doesn't scale. This is referred to as Amdahl's Law. It's like the law of diminishing returns.

Two early chips, both single cpu's, were designed to be the building blocks of massively parallel systems. These were the Inmos Transputer, and the Intel iWarp. Many other early MPS's were build from commodity cpu's, We'll take a look at these to see what made them the ideal component to build a MPS from.

Interconnection of CPU/GPU's and memory on a single chip

In this section, we address architectural approaches to coordinating the use of multiple processors. Most of these approaches will work with any underlying technology, and are useful after the maximum speed of a single processor in a given technology has been wrung out.

One approach to solving increasing complex problems with increasingly capable hardware is simply to wait. Given enough time, sufficiently complex hardware for the problem domain will emerge. However, it is increasingly apparent that software development lags hardware to the extent that software tools do not emerge until the hardware is obsolete by at least two generations. Also, the capabilities of any given hardware design will be exceeded by computational problems of interest well into the foreseeable future. At any given point of technological complexity, a cluster of coordinated processors can outperform a single processor. Thus, faced with a seemingly inexhaustible complex problem domain, along with industry emphasis on hardware development, we need to tackle both the software and the communication domains to better utilize the hardware available at any given point. Software will be discussed in section 4. Here, we want to discuss the critical issue of communications among elements.

The bottleneck to getting more than one processor to work on a given problem domain at one time is the communications. There is an upper bound in a bus-oriented, shared memory SMP systems, arising from the communication limit of the bus interconnect (a classic Shannon channel limit). Clusters of computers also suffer from an interprocessor communication limit, from the LAN-like interconnect. Some MPP's are like clusters in a box.

Embedded GPU Products

This section provides an overview of some of the embedded GPU products available commercially. This is a very fast moving market, and there are several players, each seeking to dominate it.

Nvidia started out addressing the video market, making faster and better video cards for pc's. Standardizing the architecture as a graphics processing unit, their chips found their way onto numerous motherboards as well. But, an amazing thing happened, almost unseen. User's realized their video card had more processing power than the motherboard. So they developed some software libraries and began mis-using their video hardware for computation. It was not long until multiple cards were in use, as the system scaled nicely. This approach was not lost on the tradition computer box manufacturers.

Nvidia

Cuda (Compute Unified Device Architecture) is a trademark of nVidia Corporation. It is a parallel computing platform and a programming model. It enables dramatic increases in computing performance by harnessing the power of the graphics processing unit. A CUDA program includes parallel functions (kernels) across parallel threads. The compiler organizes these threads into blocks and grids. A block is a set of concurrently executing threads that can synchronize and co-ordinate. A grid is an array of blocks. In the CUDA programming model a thread has private memory. Each block has shared memory space, as do Grids.

Threads map to processors. Each Gpu unit executes one or more grids. Each streaming multiprocessor executes one or more thread blocks, and CUDA cores, and possibly other execution engines, execute threads.

CUDA introduced a variation on the digital signal processing Multiply-Accumulate operation (AxB+C), called Fused Multiply-ADD (FMA). In traditional Multiply-Add the AxB product will be truncated, but in the FMA, all bits of the produce are retained for the ADD operation.

SMX is nVidia's term for the Streaming Microprocessor architecture. SMX has 8 instruction dispatch engines, a 32-bit register files of size 65,536, 64 kbytes of shared memory/L1 cache, and a 48k read-only data cache. This cache is reserved for data values known (by the compiler) not to change, and thus no cache writes are required. The unit also includes 192 CUDA cores, 64 double-precision arithmetic units, 32 special function units (SFU), and 32 load/store units. The CUDA cores include both integer and floating point capability. The special function units assist in transcendental computations.

Tegra refers to a family of system-on-a-chip modules from nVidia. It includes an ARM cpu, with a graphics processing unit, a southbridge and northbridge, and a memory controller. The first model was announced in 2008. The second generation unit, Tegra 2, available in 2011 and 2012, included a dual-core ARM Cortex A9, a GPU, 32 bit memory controller, and a dual 32k L1 and a 1 megabyte L2 cache. The A9 does not include the ARM SIMD extension. The Tegra 3 has a quad core ARM Cortex A9, with a 5th low power core. The quad core can power down letting the 5th core take care of easy jobs. Tegra 3 does support the SIMD extension. The GPU is enhanced. It has the same cache architecture. Tegra 4 was announced in 2013, and retains the quad-core Arm, with a 5th low power core. Again, the GPU is enhanced over the previous model. It retains the same L1 cache, but L2 doubles to 2 megabytes. The Tegra Apalis TK1 is a Tegra K1 on a plug-in module. It has a quad core Cortex A-15, 2 gigs of ram and 16 gigs of flash. It includes usb, ethernet, and RS-232. It requires 12 volts, 30 watts. The nVidia Tegra is the basis for the touchscreen units on the Tesla electric car.

The Jetson TK1 is a board-based product with an Arm Cortex A15 processor, the Kepler GPU with 192 cores, and up to 4 gigs of memory.

The nVidia Drive is a scalable AI platform targeted for Autonomous driving. It can be single chip based, or a multi-chip platform. It is targeted to Level 5 autonomous driving. The Pegasus is a self-driving enabling platform, capable of 320 TOPS performance. The Xavier reaches 30 TOPS, at 30 watts power draw. There is also the Parker AutoChauffer and autocruise that are available now. TOPS refers to a trillion (10^{12}) deep learning operations per second.

Intel

The Intel Xeon Phi is a many-core X86 architecture. The x86 part allows it to run software developed for that architecture, and that core is linked to the GPU core. In 2013, the world's faster supercomputer, the Iianhe-2 in China, was based on 48,000 Xeon-Pi's.

The Intel Knight's Landing is a second generation many-integrated core architecture, circa 2013. It contains up to 72 Atom cores, each core being 4-way multi-threaded. It supports dual AVX-512, 512-bit vector SIMD processors. Knight's Hill is the 3rd generation device. It was focused to deep learning, but was canceled in 2017. The Knight's Mill was the replacement product, coming out in December of 2017. It supports 4-way hyperthreading.

Intel implements Imagination Technologies PowerVR architecture under license. This architecture supports very high speed 3D rendering. Now in their 8th generation, some of the family members are achieving 25 gflops, with an architecture built for Apple capable of 360 Gflops.

AMD embedded Radeon

Radeon is another major manufacturer of high end GPU cards, starting in the year 2000. Radeon is now a division of AMD. They are supported by a proprietary software device driver package called Radeon Software, Crimson edition. This runs on Microsoft operating systems, or linux. There is also an open source tool, the Direct Rendering Infrastructure.

AMD's accelerated processing unit (APU) is a 64-bit CPU and graphics accelerator. It is based on the

Heterogeneous System Architecture (HSA) standard. It allows for the CPU and GPU to operate on the same bus, with shared memory. ARM is also a member of the HSA Foundation. The graphics cpu also does the floating point operations. AMD calls it the STREAM technology, and it is supported with OpenCL.

AMD's E8950MXM module uses their 4th Polaris architecture, of which there are multiple instantiations. AMD will release a follow-on 6th gen architecture in 2019.

Curtis Wright

Curtis Wright is an innovator in getting supercomputing class power in ruggedized embedded systems. They use Intel-based multi-processor boards with AVX, GPGPU co-processors, Xilinx FPGAs, SRIO and Ethernet switching. Their VPX approach optimizes the VMEbus. They also address power issues as well as cooling. The company, originally an aircraft manufacturer founded in 1929, has diversified.

Open Source versus Proprietary

This is a topic we need to discuss before we get very far into software. It is not a technical topic, but concerns your right to use (and/or own, modify) software. It's those software licenses you click to agree with, and never read. That's what the intellectual property lawyers are betting on.

Software and software tools are available in proprietary and open source versions. Open source software is free and widely available, and may be incorporated into your system. It is available under license, which generally says that you can use it, but derivative products must be made available under the same license. This presents a problem if it is mixed with purchased, licensed commercial software, or a level of exclusivity is required. Major government agencies such as the Department of Defense and NASA have policies related to the use of Open Source software.

Adapting a commercial or open source operating system to a particular problem domain can be tricky. Usually, the commercial operating systems need to be used "as-is" and the source code is not available. The software can usually be configured between well-defined limits, but there will be no visibility of the internal workings. For the open source situation, there will be a multitude of source code modules and libraries that can be configured and customized, but the process is complex. The user can also write new modules in this case.

Large corporations or government agencies sometimes have problems incorporating open source products into their projects. Open Source did not fit the model of how they have done business traditionally. They are issues and lingering doubts. Many Federal agencies have developed Open Source policies. NASA has created an open source license, the NASA Open Source Agreement (NOSA), to address these issues. It has released software under this license, but the Free Software Foundation had some issues with the terms of the license. The Open Source Initiative (www.opensource.org) maintains the definition of Open Source, and certifies licenses such as the NOSA.

The GNU General Public License (GPL) is the most widely used free software license. It guarantees end users the freedoms to use, study, share, copy, and modify the software. Software that ensures that these rights are retained is called free software. The license was originally written by Richard Stallman of the Free Software Foundation (FSF) for the GNU project in 1989. The GPL is a *copyleft* license, which means that derived works can only be distributed under the same license terms. This is in distinction to permissive free software licenses, of which the BSD licenses are the standard examples. Copyleft is in counterpoint to traditional copyright. Proprietary software "poisons" free software, and cannot be included or integrated with it, without abandoned the GPL. The GPL covers the GNU/linux operating systems and most of the GNU/linux-based applications.

A Vendor's software tools and operating system or application code is usually proprietary intellectual property. It is unusual to get the source code to examine, at least without binding legal documents and additional funds. Along with this, you do get the vendor support. An alternative is open source code, which is in the public domain. There are a series of licenses covering open source code usage, including the Creative Commons License, the gnu public license, copyleft, and others. Open Source describes a collaborative environment for development and testing. Use of open source code carries with it an implied responsibility to "pay back" to the community. Open Source is not necessarily free.

The Open source philosophy is sometimes at odds with the rigidized procedures evolved to ensure software performance and reliability. Offsetting this is the increased visibility into the internals of the software packages, and control over the entire software package. Besides application code, operating systems such as GNU/linux and bsd can be open source. The programming language Python is open source. The popular web server Apache is also open source.

Parallel Software Tools

Matlab has a product, GPU Coder, that generates optimized code for the cuda. It makes use of the nVidia libraries. With the Embedded coder software, the numerical behavior of the code can be characterized. Matlab also supports Deep Learning on the Cuda.

The Heterogeneous System Architecture (HSA) Foundation is involved in open source software development for high performance architectures, as well as the hardware specifications for the architecture. It is a collaboration of various hardware and software companies, National Labs, and Universities. The HSA Foundation is a member of the Linux foundation.

PNN

The probabilistic neural network is a technique for classification of data, and pattern recognition. It is used to reduce large sets of raw data to useful information. It dates from 1966, but wasn't applied until sufficient computation resources were available to host the algorithm. It relies on training sets.

OpenMP

OpenMP represents an API for shared memory multi-platform, multiprocessing, It supports most architectures, including nVidia. It is open source, from the OpenMP Architecture Review Board. It is essentially an implementation of multi-threading, where the threads of execution can be mapped to compute resources. Assigning threads to processors is done at run time. The first version of the software appeared in 1997, for the Fortran language. The c/c++ languages are now supported. A large number of compilers support OpenMP.

Nvidia

Nvidia has a series of applications and libraries for their Cuda product. These include cuDNN, for deep neural networks, the Toolkit, cuSolver, and cuBLAS. DNN is a set of libraries that are optimized for the gpu architecture. NVIDIA also offers a SDK for deep learning. The TensorRT product is targeted to deep learning applications. It is based on their Volta GPU.

Applications

What applications are enabled by embedded GPUs? This section will discuss some of these.

High Performance Embedded Computing (HPEC)

High performance embedded computing brings supercomputer class performance to the embedded world. This implies not only fast computation and throughput, but fast I/O as well. There is in place a series of software standards called Open Standard software solutions for high performance computing. We can do a lot more computation with multiple GPU's. One of the big drivers (no pun intended) is self-driving cars and trucks.

Embedded AI

Embedded artificial intelligence and embedded deep learning are being deployed. Both require supercomputer-level computing, and we used to get that from the Cloud, but that's not a problem in the embedded world today. One application that has been deployed is Apple's Face ID, a bio-metric authentication system that runs on a phone. It is hosted on a custom System-on-a-Chip architecture, and is capable of 600 giga-operations per second. The chip is named the A11 Bionic engine. The system uses the front facing camera to map 30,000 points in the infrared spectrum. Apple has a library of apps for this, including the iOS imaging SDK. ARM developed the hardware, and is able to use it on its own generic designs. In the ARM context, it is called DynamIQ, and runs on the ARM Cortex A chips.

Google is implementing a platform to host deep learning algorithms on ARM. At the moment, the hard work is done in the Cloud, but this has issues with privacy. When the relevant search is done on your device, it is easier to control the security aspects. A company called Reality AI is developing machine learning software libraries for embedded use.

Voice controlled assistants such as Amazon's Echo and Google Home now use cloud services to parse the verbal input. Current generation GPU's have the ability to do this, in situ. What the local units will not have, but will have access to, are the large databases, now hosted in the Cloud.

Deep Learning

Deep learning algorithms, based on advanced GPU hardware platforms and neural network algorithms are changing the way large data sets are processed. This is very applicable to vision data, in the context of self-driving cars, and for mobile robot systems. Path planning in a cluttered environment, with a high cost of failure, are the topics. Now, the algorithms are proven, and the hardware can support their real-time behavior.

The Neuromorphic model, based on Carver Mead's work in the 1980's, is being applied, as it is now computationally feasible to implement. The model is based on electronic analog systems mimicking the nervous system. Now, the systems can be digital, analog, or a hybrid of both.

Predictive Analytics

Predictive analytics is based on modeling, machine learning, and data collection/mining to analyze current conditions to predict future conditions. As an example, car speed, input from multiple cameras, GPS position, to calculate the next step for a self-driving car. The next step is to update the prediction versus the reality, allowing the system to learn in realtime. Predictive Analytics can be run on streaming data, such as we might get from a digital camera. There is a large set of predictive analysis tools available in Open Source and commercial format. Predictive Analytics is trying to predict the future, which, for short time horizons, you can do. Usually. The key part is to compare the prediction to reality, and learn from the experience. This is enabled with high end GPU's.

Deep Neural Network

A deep neural network learns from the dataset. We do not influence how it learns. A convolutional neural network is used with images and video. It does feature detection. For example, it could use the owner's face as a password for his/her cellphone. You can actually buy a pre-trained network, which has been exposed to vast image data sets. Deep learning requires both access to very large data sets, and massive computational resources. It has passed the point where the deep learning based image recognition has surpassed human abilities. Automotive DLL's are now using continuously updating 360 degree views.

Embedded GPU's for Robotics

Embedded GPU's have the ability of making mobile robot systems much more capable. The trade-off is, they will require more power. If the robot relies on a cloud service for image recognition, for example, the cost of communication must be taken into account, and even whether communication is possible. The robot might be exploring a mine, for example. The power problem involves the power cost of mobility and computation. As was seen with the early Mars Rovers, it took more power to compute the next move, than to actually accomplish it.

In addition, a mobile platform needs to recharge it's batteries now and then, with the options being solar, and returning to a charging station. As technology progresses, we will get better batteries, and lower power GPU's.

Afterword

As electronics follows the path of Moore's law, and increases in complexity, we are seeing what a few years ago was thought to be impossible except by magic. The technologies feed upon each other to produce more complex systems of systems. The key will be how to manage these riches.

Bibliography

Aiken, Ales; Banerjee, Utpal *Instruction Level Parallelism*, Springer, 1st ed, 2016, ISBN-978-1489977953.

Bakowski, Przemyslaw *A Practical Introduction to Parallel Programming on multi-core and many-core Embedded Systems*, 2014, ASIN-B00MKWXOKY.

Barlas, Gerassimos *Multicore and GPU Programming: An Integrated Approach,* Morgan Kaufmann, 1st ed, 2014, ISBN-978-0124171374.

Cai, Yiyu; See, Simon *GPU Computing and Applications*, Springer, 2015, ISBN-978-9811013607.

Chapman, Barbara, et al *Parallel Computing: From Multicores and Gpu's to Petascale* (Advances in Parallel Computing), 2010, ISBN-10-1607505290.

Cook, Shane *CUDA Programming: A Developer's Guide to Parallel Computing with GPUs,* 1st edition, Morgan Kaufmann, 2012, ISBN-978-0124159334.

Couturier, Raphael (Ed) *Designing Scientific Applications on GPUs* (Chapman & Hall/CRC Numerical Analysis and Scientific Computing Series), 1st Edition, ISBN-1466571624.

Fadhil Heba M.;Younis, Mohammed I.A *Multithreading*

Implementation of RSA Algorithm on Multicore and GPU, 2015, ISBN-3659748595.

Games, Richard A. *Real-Time Embedded High Performance Computing: Communications Scheduling,* 1995, ASIN-B00HCTZC3M.

Hennessy, John L. Patterson, and David A. *Computer Architecture, Sixth Edition: A Quantitative Approach* (The Morgan Kaufmann Series in Computer Architecture and Design), 6th ed, 2017, ISBN-0128119055.

Jaraweh, Yaser, et al "GPU-based Personal Supercomputing," 2013, IEEE, Applied Electrical Engineering and Computing Technologies (AEECT).

Jeffers, Jim; Reinders, James *High Performance Parallelism Pearls Volume Two: Multicore and Many-core Programming Approaches*, 2015, ISBN-0128038195.

Keller, Rainer; Kramer, David *Facing the Multicore-Challenge III: Aspects of New Paradigms and Technologies in Parallel Computing* (Lecture Notes in Computer Science), 2013, ISBN-3642358926.

Kepner, Jeremy *High Performance Embedded Computing Software Initiative (HPEC-SI)*, 2004, ASIN-B00NYH2NQ0.

Kindratenko, Volodymyr (Ed) *Numerical Computations*

with GPUs, Springer, 2014, ISBN-978-3319065472.
Kindratenko, Volodymyr V. et all, "GPU Clusters for High-Performance Computing,"
avail:
www.ncsa.illinois.edu/People/kindr/papers/ppac09_paper.pdf

Kirk, David B.; Hwu, Wen-mei W. *Programming Massively Parallel Processors: A Hands-on Approach,* 1st Edition, ISBN-0128119861.

Lowndes, Alison B. *Deep Learning with GPUs: For the beginner,* 2016, ISBN-3659850284.

Natloff, Norman *Parallel Computing for Data Science: With Examples in R, C++ and CUDA* (Chapman & Hall/CRC The R Series), 2015, ISBN-1466587016.

Martinez, David R.; Bond, Robert A. *High Performance Embedded Computing Handbook: A Systems Perspective,* 2008, ISBN-084937197X.

Mead, Carver *Analog VLSI and Neural Systems,* 1989, ISBN-0201059924.

Mead, Carver; Ismail, Mohammed *Analog VLSI Implementation of Neural Systems,* 1989, ISBN-0792390407.

Rahman, Rezaur *Intel Xeon Phi Coprocessor Architecture and Tools: The Guide for Application*

Developers, 1st edition, 2013, ISBN-1430259264.

Schmidt, Bertil *Bioinformatics: High Performance Parallel Computer Architectures* (Embedded Multi-Core Systems), 2010, ISBN-1439814880.

Stakem, Patrick H., *Graphics Processing Units, an overview,* 2017, PRRB Publishing, ISBN-1520879695.

Stakem, Patrick H. *Multicore Computer Architecture*, 2014, PRRB Publishing, ISBN-1520241372.

Stakem, Patrick H. *Massively Parallel Microprocessor Systems*, 1997, PRRB Publishing, ISBN-1520250061.

Stakem, Patrick H. *Embedded Computer Systems, Volume 1, Introduction and Architecture,* PRRB Publishing 2013, ISBN-1520215959.

Stakem, Patrick H. *The Hardware and Software Architecture of the Transputer,* 2011, PRRB Publishing, ISBN-152020681X.

Stakem, Patrick H. *Computer Architecture & Programming of the Intel x86 Family, 2013,* PRRB, ISBN – 978-1520263724.

Stakem, Patrick H. *Floating Point Computation*, 2013, PRRB, ISBN-152021619X.

Storti, Duane; Yurtoglu, Mete, CUDA for Engineers: An

Introduction to High-Performance Parallel Computing, Addison Wesley Professional, 1st ed, 2015, 978-0134177410. ISBN-1520215959.

Suh, Jung W., Kim, Youngmin, *Accelerating MATLAB with GPU Computing: A Primer with Examples*, Morgan Kaufmann, 1st ed, 2013, ISBN-978-0124080805.

Tan, Ying *GPU-based Parallel Implementation of Swarm Intelligence Algorithms*, 2016, 1st ed, Morgan Kaufmann, ISBN-978-0128093627.

Wilt, Nicholas, The *CUDA Handbook: A Comprehensive Guide to GPU Programming,* 1st ed, Addison-Wesley Professional, ISBN-978-0321809469.

Yuen, David A. (ed) *GPU Solutions to Multi-scale Problems in Science and Engineering*, Springer, 2013, ISBN-978-3642164040

Wang, Endong *High-Performance Computing on the Intel Xeon Phi: How to Fully Exploit MIC Architectures*, 2014, ISBN-3319064851.

Wolf, Marilyn *High-Performance Embedded Computing, Second Edition: Applications in Cyber-Physical Systems and Mobile Computing*, 2nd ed, Morgan Kaufmann, 2014, ISBN-0124105114.

Resources

GPU Computing for embedded applications, avail: http://www.ices.kth.se/upload/events/99/20a331d424114f dfb04238af9938b3fd.pdf

http://www.amd.com/en-us/products/embedded/graphics

http://spectrum.ieee.org/static/chip-hall-of-fame

NASA Space Technology Roadmaps and Priorities: Restoring NASA's Technological Edge and Paving the Way for a New Era in Space, Aeronautics and Space Engineering Board, Steering Committee (2012), Avail: https://www.sti.nasa.gov/

https://www.curtisswrightds.com/products/cots-boards/processor-cards/software-ip/openhpec.html

Wikipedia, various.

Glossary of terms

1's complement – signed integer format that forms the negative by logically inverting all the bits. There are, unfortunately, 2 different values of zero.

2's complement – signed integer format in which a negative is formed by doing the 1's complement, and then adding 1. There is only 1 representation of zero.

2-d – two dimensional.

3-d – three dimensional.

Accumulator – a register to hold numeric values during and after an operation.

Actuator – device which converts a control signal to a mechanical action.

Ada – a programming language named after Ada Augusta, Countess of Lovelace, and daughter of Lord Byron; arguably, the first programmer. Collaborator with Charles Babbage.

A/D, ADC – analog to digital converter.

ANN – artificial neural networks.

ASIC - application specific integrated circuit

ALU – arithmetic-logic unit, does arithmetic and logical operations on data.

AMD – Advanced Micro Devices (Company).

Analog – concerned with continuous values.

ANSI – American National Standards Institute.

AOP – always on processor.

API – applications program interface, a set of routines, protocols, and tools for building software applications.

APU – accelerated processing unit (AMD).

ARM – originally, Acorn Risc Machines. Now, ARM Holdings, the owner of the ARM architecture IP.

ASCII - American Standard Code for Information Interchange, a 7-bit code; developed for teleprinters.

ASIC – application specific integrated circuit, custom or semicustom.

ASIN – Amazon standard inventory number.

Assembly language – low level programming language specific to a particular ISA.

Async – asynchronous; using different clocks.

ATCA- Advanced Telecomm Computing Architecture (spec).

AVX – advanced vector extensions (Intel).

BBC - British Broadcasting Corporation.

Beowulf – clustering technology for Gnu-Linux-based computers.

Big-endian – data format with the most significant bit or byte at the lowest address, or transmitted first.

Big-endian - having the least significant byte in a word

on the right.

BIST – built-in self test.

Bit - the smallest unit of binary information.

Blackbox – functional device with inputs and outputs, but no detail on the internal workings.

BLOB - Binary Large Object, usually applied to data.

Bootstrap – a startup or reset process that proceeds without external intervention.

BSP – board support package; information and drivers for a specific circuit board.

Buffer – a temporary holding location for data.

Bug – an error in a program or device.

Byte - a collection of 8 bits

Cache- a small, fast memory between the processor and the main memory.

Cache coherency – process to keep the contents of multiple caches consistent,

CAN – controller area network.

CAS – column address strobe (in DRAM refreshing)

Chip – integrated circuit component.

Codec – coder/decoder. For example, for MPEG.

Configuware – equivalent of software for FPGA architectures; configuration information.

Control Flow – computer architecture involving directed

flow through the program; data dependent paths are allowed.

COP – computer operating properly.

Coprocessor – another processor to supplement the operations of the main processor. Used for floating point, video, etc. Usually relies on the main processor for instruction fetch and control.

CPU – central processing unit.

CRC – cyclic redundancy code, an error-control mechanism.

CTC – Connectionist Temporal Classification, a type of neural network.

D/A – digital to analog conversion.

DAC – digital to analog converter.

CUDA - Compute Unified Device Architecture, from Nvidia.

Dataflow – a computer architecture that allows concurrent execution; sometimes called stream processing.

Data parallelism – data distributed across nodes in a parallel architecture.

D-cache – data cache

DCT – discrete cosine transformation.

DDR – dual data rate (memory).

Deadlock – a situation in which two or more competing actions are each waiting for the other to finish, and thus neither ever does.

DCE – data communications equipment; interface to the network.

Denorm – in floating point representation, a non-zero number with a magnitude less than the smallest normal number.

Dirty bit – used to signal that the contents of a cache have changed.

DMA - direct memory addressing - I/O to/from memory without processor involvement.

DNN – deep neural network

Double word – two words; if word = 8 bits, double word = 16 bits.

DSP – Digital Signal Processing.

Dram – dynamic random access memory.

DVI – digital visual interface (for video).

Embedded system – a computer systems with limited human interfaces and performing specific tasks. Usually part of a larger system.

Epitaxial – in semiconductors, have a crystalline overlayer with a well-defined orientation.

EU – execution unit. Contains the ALU and registers, maybe the FPU.

Exception – interrupt due to internal events, such as overflow, or attempted division by zero.

Fetch/execute cycle – basic operating cycle of a

computer; fetch the instruction, execute the instruction

File – a container of information, usually stored as a one dimensional array of bytes.

Firmware – code contained in a non-volatile memory.

Fixed point – computer numeric format with a fixed number of digits or bits, and a fixed radix point.

Flag – a binary indicator.

Flash memory – a type of non-volatile memory, similar to EEprom.

Flip-flop – a circuit with two stable states; ideal for binary.

Floating Point - a scientific/engineering numeric representation scheme with a mantissa and an exponent.

FPGA – field programmable gate array.

FPU – floating point unit – does math operations on floating point formatted data.

Frame buffer – implemented in RAM, contains a bitmap and a complete frame of data.

Full duplex – communication in both directions simultaneously.

Gate – a circuit to implement a logic function; can have multiple inputs, but a single output.

Gather – loading vector data from non-contiguous memory locations.

GFLOPS - Giga (10^9) Floating Point Operations per second.

GIPS - Giga (10^9) Operations per second.

Gnu – recursive acronym; gnu (is) not unix. Operating system that is free software.

GPGPU – general purpose (computing) on graphics processing units.

GPIO – general purpose input output

GPU – graphics processing unit, ALU for graphics data. nVidia.

GPU cluster – compute nodes and fast interconnect, a classic MPMS.

GUI – Graphical User Interface.

Half-duplex – communications in two directions, but not simultaneously.

Handshake – co-ordination mechanism.

Harvard architecture – memory storage scheme with separate instructions and data.

HDMI – High Definition Multimedia Interface.

Hexadecimal – base 16 number representation.

Hexadecimal point – radix point that separates integer from fractional values of hexadecimal numbers.

Hotplug – to connect equipment without turning the power off first.

HP – Hewlett-Packard Company. Instrumentation and computers.

HPC – high performance computing.

HPEC – high performance embedded computing; also, high performance extreme computing

HSA – Heterogeneous System Architecture.

Hypervisor – virtual machine manager. Can manage multiple operating systems.

I2C – Inter-Integrated Circuit interface. A short-range serial link, using a multi-master bus.

I-cache – instruction cache.

I^2C – inter-integrated circuit; a multi-master serial single-ended computer bus invented by Philips.

Icon – a graphical representation or pictogram.

IDCT – inverse discrete cosine transformation.

IDE – Integrated development environment for software or configware.

IEEE- Institute of Electronic and Electronic Engineers.

IEEE-754 – standard for floating point representation and operations.

Infinity - the largest number that can be represented in the number system.

Integer – the natural numbers, zero, and the negatives of the natural numbers.

Interrupt – an asynchronous event to signal a need for attention (example: the phone rings).

Interrupt vector – entry in a table pointing to an interrupt service routine; indexed by interrupt number.

I/O – Input-output from the computer to external devices, or a user interface.

IP – intellectual property; also internet protocol.

IP core – IP describing a chip design that can be licensed to be used in an FPGA or ASIC.

ISA – instruction set architecture.

ISBN – International Standard Book Number.

ISO – International Standards Organization.

ISP – Image System Pipeline (ARM).

ISR – interrupt service routine, a subroutine that handles a particular interrupt event.

Java – programming language that targets the Java Virtual Machine.

Jazelle – direct execution of Java bytecodes, as opposed to execution in the Java Virtual Machine.

JPEG - Joint Photographic Experts Group.

JTAG – Joint Test Action Group; industry group that lead to IEEE 1149.1, Standard Test Access Port and Boundary-Scan Architecture.

Junction – in semiconductors, the boundary interface of the n-type and p-type material.

JVM – Java Virtual Machine – software that allows any architecture to execute Java bytecodes by emulation.

Kernel – main portion of the operating system. Interface between the applications and the hardware.

Kilo – a prefix for 10^3 or 2^{10}

L1 – cache closest to the CPU.

L2 – cache next in line.

LAN – local area network.

Latency – time delay.

LCD – liquid crystal display.

LED – light emitting diode.

Linux – unix-like operating system developed by Linus Torvalds; open source.

List – a data structure.

Little-endian having the least significant byte of a word on the right.

Logical operation – AND, OR, Exclusive OR, (and their inverses) and Negate.

Loop-unrolling – optimization of a loop for speed at the cost of space.

LRU – least recently used; an algorithm for item replacement in a cache.

LSB – least significant bit or byte.

LSTM – long short-term memory for a recurrent neural network.

LUT – look up table.

MAC – multiply-accumulate, a primitive operation in signal processing; also, media access control.

LUT – look up table.

Mainframe – a computer you can't lift.

Malware – malicious software; virus, worm, Trojan, spyware, adware, and such.

Mantissa – significant digits (as opposed to the exponent) of a floating point value.

Master-slave – control process with one element in charge. Master status may be exchanged among elements.

MC – motion compensation.

MCM – multi-chip module

Master-slave – control process with one element in charge. Master status may be exchanged among elements.

Memory leak – when a program uses memory resources but does not return them, leading to a lack of available memory.

Memory scrubbing – detecting and correcting bit errors.

Mesh – a highly connected network.

MESI – modified, exclusive, shared, invalid state of a cache coherency protocol.

Metaprogramming – programs that produce or modify other programs.

MIC – (Intel) Many Integrated Core architecture.

Microcode – hardware level data structures to translate machine instructions into sequences of circuit level operations.

Microcontroller – microprocessor with included memory and/or I/O.

Microkernel – operating system which is not monolithic. So functions execute in user space.

Microprocessor – a monolithic CPU on a chip.

Microprogramming – modifying the microcode.

Middleware – software layer between the application and the operating system, providing services.

MIL-STD-1553 – military standard (US) for a serial communications bus for avionics.

MIMD – multiple instruction, multiple data

Minicomputer – smaller than a mainframe, larger than a pc.

Minix – Unix-like operating system; free and open source.

MIPS – millions of instructions per second; sometimes used as a measure of throughput.

MMU - memory management unit, translates virtual to physical addresses.

MMX – (Intel) multimedia extensions (to the instruction set and data format).

MPE – Media Processing Engine.

MPEG – motion picture experts group – standards for audio and video compression and transmission.

MPMS – massively parallel microprocessor system.

MPU – memory protection unit – like an MMU, but

without address translation.

MRAM – Magnetorestrictive random access memory. Non-volatile memory approach using magnetic storage elements and integrated circuit fabrication techniques.

MSB – most significant bit or byte.

Multicore – multiple processing cores on one substrate or chip; need not be identical.

Multiplex – combining signals on a communication channel by sampling.

Mutex – a data structure and methodology for mutual exclusion.

NaN not-a-number (bit pattern used for status in floating point).

NEON – instruction set for SIMD processing (ARM).

NAND – negated (or inverse) AND function.

NASA – National Aeronautics and Space Administration.

NDA – non-disclosure agreement; legal agreement protecting IP.

Neuristor – an electronic circuit that mimics neuron behavior.

Neuromorphic – implementing neural/biological systems.

Nibble – 4 bits, ½ byte.

NIST – National Institute of Standards and Technology (US), previously, National Bureau of Standards.

NMI – non-maskable interrupt; cannot be ignored by the software.

NOP – no operation.

NOR – negated (or inverse) OR function

Normalized number – in the proper format for floating point representation.

Northbridge – a custom logic element that handles all of the cpu interfacing to memory and I/O. See also southbridge,

NRE – non-recurring engineering; one-time costs for a project.

Null modem – acting as two modems, wired back to back. Artifact of the RS-232 standard.

NUMA – non-uniform memory access for multiprocessors; local and global memory access protocol.

NVM – non-volatile memory.

Nyquist rate – in communications, the minimum sampling rate, equal to twice the highest frequency in the signal.

OBD – On-Board diagnostics;a state-of-health system

Octal – base 8 number.

Off-the-shelf – commercially available; not custom.

OMAP – Open Multimedia Applications Platform. (Texas Instruments)

Opcode – part of a machine language instruction that

specifies the operation to be performed.

Open source – methodology for hardware or software development with free distribution and access.

Opcode – part of a machine language instruction that specifies the operation to be performed.

OpenHPEC – Open high performance embedded computing software standards.

ORNL – Oak Ridge National Lab, U.S. National Laboratory of the Department of Energy.

OSI – Open systems interconnect model for networking, from ISO.

Overflow - the result of an arithmetic operation exceeds the capacity of the destination.

Packet – a small container; a block of data on a network.

Paging – memory management technique using fixed size memory blocks.

Paradigm – a pattern or model

Paradigm shift – a change from one paradigm to another. Disruptive or evolutionary.

Parallel – multiple operations or communication proceeding simultaneously.

Parity – an error detecting mechanism involving an extra check bit in the word.

Pascal – a programming language (circa 1970).

PC – personal computer, politically correct, program counter.

PCB – printed circuit board.

PCI – peripheral interconnect interface (bus).

PCIe – Peripheral Component Interconnect Express. A serial bus.

PCM – pulse code modulation.

PE - processor element, usually consisting of cpu, memory, I/O.

Peta - 10^{15} or 2^{50}

Petaflops – 10^{15} floating point operations per second.

Pinout – mapping of signals to I/O pins of a device.

Pipeline – operations in serial, assembly-line fashion.

Pixel – picture element; smallest addressable element on a display or a sensor.

PLD– programmable logic device; generic gate-level part that can be programmed for a function.

PMOS – positive metal oxide semiconductor, in which the carriers are positively charged.

Posix – portable operating system interface, IEEE standard.

PPU - Physics processing unit; does rigid and non-rigid body dynamics, fluid dynamics, finite element analysis, etc. GPU-based.

PROM – programmable read-only memory.

Pullup – a resistor to tie a signal point to + voltage to establish level, and the transistor has no drive capability. a logic state. Used with an open-collector transistor architecture. Without the pullup, the output of the transistors floats to a random voltage

PWM – pulse width modulation.

Python – programming language.

Quad word – four words. If word = 16 bits, quad word is 64 bits.

Queue – first in, first out data buffer structure; hardware of software.

RAID – random array of inexpensive disks; using commodity disk drives to build large storage arrays.

Radix point – separates integer and fractional parts of a real number.

RAM – random access memory; any item can be access in the same time as any other.

RAS – Row address strobe, in dram refresh.

Rasterization – process in which geometric shapes are converted to pixels, for display.

Register – temporary storage location for a data item.

Reset – signal and process that returns the hardware to a known, defined state.

RISC – reduced instruction set computer.

RNN - recurrent neural network.

SATA – serial ATA, a storage media interconnect.

Sandbox – an isolated and controlled environment to run

untested or potentially malicious code.

SCADA – Supervisory Control and Data Acquisition – for industrial control systems.

Script – a program for an interpreter. Used to automate tasks.

Scatter – storing a vector data in non-contiguous memory locations.

SDK – system (or, software) development kit.

SDR – software defined radio.

SDRAM – synchronous dynamic random access memory.

Segmentation – dividing a network or memory into sections.

Self-modifying code – computer code that modifies itself as it run; hard to debug

Semiconductor – material with electrical characteristics between conductors and insulators; basis of current technology processor and memory devices.

Semaphore –signaling element among processes.

Sensor – a device that converts a physical observable quantity or event to a signal.

Serial – bit by bit.

Server – a computer running services on a network.

Set-top box – embedded system to provide interface to a television from cable and internet.

SFU – Special Function Unit.

Shannon limit – in communications theory, the theorem that it is possible to communicate digital data nearly error-free up to a maximum rate through the channel, based on the noise. This result was presented by Claude Shannon in 1948.

Shift – move one bit position to the left or right in a word.

Signed number – representation with a value and a numeric sign.

SIMD – single instruction, multiple data.

Simm – single in-line memory module.

SIMT - Single Instruction, Multiple Thread

Sign-Magnitude – data format which has a sign bit, and an integer value.

SIMD – Single Instruction, Multiple Data. An operation on Vector data types.

SIMT – single instruction, multiple thread.

SMP - 	symmetric multi processor, or processing.

SMX – Streaming Microprocessor architecture, nVidia.

SOC – system on chip.

Software – set of instructions and data to tell a computer what to do.

Southbridge – custom logic that implements the I/O functionality. See also north bridge

SMP – symmetric multiprocessing.

Snoop – monitor packets in a network, or data in a cache

SPI – Serial Peripheral Interface (bus): short distance, synchronous serial.

SRAM – static random access memory.

SSE - Streaming SIMD Extensions (SSE) – Intel.

Stack – first in, last out data structure. Can be hardware or software.

Stack pointer – a reference pointer to the top of the stack.

State machine – model of sequential processes.

Superscalar – computer with instruction-level parallelism, by replication of resources.

SWD – serial wire debug.

Synchronous – using the same clock to coordinate operations.

System – a collection of interacting elements and relationships with a specific behavior.

System of Systems – a complex collection of systems with pooled resources.

Table – data structure. Can be multi-dimensional.

TCP/IP – transmission control protocol/internet protocol; layered set of protocols for networks.

Tera - 10^{12} or 2^{40}

Test-and-set – coordination mechanism for multiple processes that allows reading to a location and writing it in a non-interruptible manner.

Texturing – computing the colors of rendered surfaces.

TFU – texture filtering unit.

Thread – smallest independent set of instructions managed by a multiprocessing operating system

TLB – translation lookaside buffer – a cache of addresses.

TMR – Triple Modular Redundancy; an error control mechanism using redundant components.

TOPS - trillion (10^{12}) deep learning operations per second.

TPU – tensor processing unit.

Transceiver – receiver and transmitter in one box.

Transducer – a device that converts one form of energy to another (example: the Grand Coulee Dam).

Transputer – a microcomputer on a chip by Inmos Corp., circa 1980. Innovative communication mechanism using serial links.

TRAP – exception or fault handling mechanism in a computer; an operating system component.

Triplicate – using three copies (of hardware, software, , power supplies, etc.). for redundancy and error control.

Tri-state – logic with 0, 1, and a high impedance for output port to allow line sharing.

Truncate – discard. Cutoff, make shorter

TTL – transistor-transistor logic in digital integrated

circuits. (1963)

UART – Universal Asynchronous Receiver-Transmitter.

UDP – User datagram protocol; part of the Internet Protocol.

USART – universal synchronous (or) asynchronous receiver/transmitter.

UPS – uninterruptable power supply. Backup power source.

USB – universal serial bus.

Unsigned number – a number without a numeric sign.

Underflow – the result of an arithmetic operation is smaller than the smallest representable number.

Vector – a collection of similar data in a one dimensional array.

Vector processor – a unit that does operations on vectors of data.

VHDL- very high level description language; a language to describe integrated circuits and asic/ fpga's.

VIA – vertical conducting pathway through an insulating layer in a semiconductor.

Virtual memory – memory management technique using address translation.

Virtualization – creating a virtual resource from available physical resources.

Virus – malignant computer program.

VLIW – very long instruction word – mechanism for

parallelism.

Von Neumann computer architecture, control flow, data and instructions share memory

VPU – Vision processing unit (ATI Technologies); a GPU.

Watchcat – watches the watchdog

Watchdog – hardware/software function to sanity check the hardware, software, and process; applies corrective action if a fault is detected; fail-safe mechanism.

Wiki – the Hawaiian word for "quick." Refers to a collaborative content website.

Word – a collection of bits of any size; does not have to be a power of two.

Write-back – cache organization where the data is not written to main memory until the cache location is needed for re-use.

Write-only – of no interest.

Write-through – all cache writes also go to memory.

X86 – Intel -16, -32, 64-bit ISA.

Xen – Hypervisor, U. Cambridge.

XOR – exclusive OR; either but not both.

Zero address – architecture using implicit addressing, like a stack.

If you enjoyed this book, you might also be interested in some of these.

Stakem, Patrick H. *16-bit Microprocessors, History and Architecture*, 2013 PRRB Publishing, ISBN-1520210922.

Stakem, Patrick H. *4- and 8-bit Microprocessors, Architecture and History*, 2013, PRRB Publishing, ISBN-152021572X,

Stakem, Patrick H. *Apollo's Computers,* 2014, PRRB Publishing, ISBN-1520215800.

Stakem, Patrick H. *The Architecture and Applications of the ARM Microprocessors,* 2013, PRRB Publishing, ISBN-1520215843.

Stakem, Patrick H. *Earth Rovers: for Exploration and Environmental Monitoring,* 2014, PRRB Publishing, ISBN-152021586X.

Stakem, Patrick H. *Embedded Computer Systems, Volume 1, Introduction and Architecture*, 2013, PRRB Publishing, ISBN-1520215959.

Stakem, Patrick H. *The History of Spacecraft Computers from the V-2 to the Space Station*, 2013, PRRB Publishing, ISBN-1520216181.

Stakem, Patrick H. *Floating Point Computation*, 2013, PRRB Publishing, ISBN-152021619X.

Stakem, Patrick H. *Architecture of Massively Parallel Microprocessor Systems*, 2011, PRRB Publishing, ISBN-1520250061.

Stakem, Patrick H. *Multicore Computer Architecture,* 2014, PRRB Publishing, ISBN-1520241372.

Stakem, Patrick H. *Personal Robots*, 2014, PRRB Publishing, ISBN-1520216254.

Stakem, Patrick H. *RISC Microprocessors, History and Overview,* 2013, PRRB Publishing, ISBN-1520216289.

Stakem, Patrick H. *Robots and Telerobots in Space Applications*, 2011, PRRB Publishing, ISBN-1520210361.

Stakem, Patrick H. *The Saturn Rocket and the Pegasus Missions, 1965,* 2013, PRRB Publishing, ISBN-1520209916.

Stakem, Patrick H. *Visiting the NASA Centers, and Locations of Historic Rockets & Spacecraft,* 2017, PRRB Publishing, ISBN-1549651205.

Stakem, Patrick H. *Microprocessors in Space*, 2011, PRRB Publishing, ISBN-1520216343.

Stakem, Patrick H. Computer *Virtualization and the Cloud*, 2013, PRRB Publishing, ISBN-152021636X.

Stakem, Patrick H. *What's the Worst That Could Happen? Bad Assumptions, Ignorance, Failures and Screw-ups in Engineering Projects, 2014*, PRRB Publishing, ISBN-1520207166.

Stakem, Patrick H. *Computer Architecture & Programming of the Intel x86 Family, 2013*, PRRB Publishing, ISBN-1520263724.

Stakem, Patrick H. *The Hardware and Software Architecture of the Transputer*, 2011,PRRB Publishing, ISBN-152020681X.

Stakem, Patrick H. *Mainframes, Computing on Big Iron*, 2015, PRRB Publishing, ISBN- 1520216459.

Stakem, Patrick H. *Spacecraft Control Centers*, 2015, PRRB Publishing, ISBN-1520200617.

Stakem, Patrick H. *Embedded in Space, 2015*, PRRB Publishing, ISBN-1520215916.

Stakem, Patrick H. *A Practitioner's Guide to RISC Microprocessor Architecture*, Wiley-Interscience, 1996, ISBN-0471130184.

Stakem, Patrick H. *Cubesat Engineering*, PRRB

Publishing, 2017, ISBN-1520754019.

Stakem, Patrick H. *Cubesat Operations*, PRRB Publishing, 2017, ISBN-152076717X.

Stakem, Patrick H. *Interplanetary Cubesats*, PRRB Publishing, 2017, ISBN-1520766173 .

Stakem, Patrick H. Cubesat Constellations, Clusters, and Swarms, Stakem, PRRB Publishing, 2017, ISBN-1520767544.

Stakem, Patrick H. *Graphics Processing Units, an overview,* 2017, PRRB Publishing, ISBN-1520879695.

Stakem, Patrick H. *Intel Embedded and the Arduino-101, 2017,* PRRB Publishing, ISBN-1520879296.

Stakem, Patrick H. *Orbital Debris, the problem and the mitigation,* 2018, PRRB Publishing, ISBN-1980466483.

Stakem, Patrick H. *Manufacturing in Space*, 2018, PRRB Publishing, ISBN-1977076041.

Stakem, Patrick H. *NASA's Ships and Planes*, 2018, PRRB Publishing, ISBN-1977076823.

Stakem, Patrick H. *Space Tourism*, 2018, PRRB Publishing, ISBN-1977073506.

Stakem, Patrick H. *STEM – Data Storage and Communications*, 2018, PRRB Publishing, ISBN-1977073115.

Stakem, Patrick H. *In-Space Robotic Repair and Servicing*, 2018, PRRB Publishing, ISBN-1980478236.

Stakem, Patrick H. *Introducing Weather in the pre-K to 12 Curricula, A Resource Guide for Educators*, 2017, PRRB Publishing, ISBN-1980638241.

Stakem, Patrick H. *Introducing Astronomy in the pre-K to 12 Curricula, A Resource Guide for Educators*, 2017, PRRB Publishing, ISBN-198104065X.
Also available in a Brazilian Portuguese edition, ISBN-1983106127.

Stakem, Patrick H. *Deep Space Gateways, the Moon and Beyond*, 2017, PRRB Publishing, ISBN-1973465701.

Stakem, Patrick H. *Exploration of the Gas Giants, Space Missions to Jupiter, Saturn, Uranus, and Neptune*, PRRB Publishing, 2018, ISBN-9781717814500.

Stakem, Patrick H. *Crewed Spacecraft*, 2017, PRRB Publishing, ISBN-1549992406.

Stakem, Patrick H. *Rocketplanes to Space*, 2017, PRRB

Publishing, ISBN-1549992589.

Stakem, Patrick H. *Crewed Space Stations,* 2017, PRRB Publishing, ISBN-1549992228.

Stakem, Patrick H. *Enviro-bots for STEM: Using Robotics in the pre-K to 12 Curricula, A Resource Guide for Educators,* 2017, PRRB Publishing, ISBN-1549656619.

Stakem, Patrick H. *STEM-Sat, Using Cubesats in the pre-K to 12 Curricula, A Resource Guide for Educators*, 2017, ISBN-1549656376.

Stakem, Patrick H. *Lunar Orbital Platform-Gateway*, 2018, PRRB Publishing, ISBN-1980498628.

Stakem, Patrick H. *Embedded GPU's*, 2018, PRRB Publishing, ISBN- 1980476497.

Stakem, Patrick H. *Mobile Cloud Robotics*, 2018, PRRB Publishing, ISBN- 1980488088.

Stakem, Patrick H. *Extreme Environment Embedded Systems,* 2017, PRRB Publishing, ISBN-1520215967.

Stakem, Patrick H. *What's the Worst, Volume-2*, 2018, ISBN-1981005579.

Stakem, Patrick H., *Spaceports*, 2018, ISBN-

1981022287.

Stakem, Patrick H., *Space Launch Vehicles*, 2018, ISBN-1983071773.

Stakem, Patrick H. *Mars*, 2018, ISBN-1983116902.

Stakem, Patrick H. *X-86, 40th Anniversary ed*, 2018, ISBN-1983189405.

Stakem, Patrick H. *Lunar Orbital Platform-Gateway*, 2018, PRRB Publishing, ISBN-1980498628.

Stakem, Patrick H. *Space Weather*, 2018, ISBN-1723904023.

Stakem, Patrick H. *STEM-Engineering Process*, 2017, ISBN-1983196517.

Stakem, Patrick H. *Space Telescopes*, 2018, PRRB Publishing, ISBN-1728728568.

Stakem, Patrick H. *Exoplanets*, 2018, PRRB Publishing, ISBN-9781731385055.

Stakem, Patrick H. *Planetary Defense*, 2018, PRRB Publishing, ISBN-9781731001207.

Patrick H. Stakem *Exploration of the Asteroid Belt*, 2018, PRRB Publishing, ISBN-1731049846.

Patrick H. Stakem *Terraforming*, 2018, PRRB Publishing, ISBN-1790308100.

Patrick H. Stakem, *Martian Railroad,* 2019, PRRB Publishing, ISBN-1794488243.

Patrick H. Stakem, *Exoplanets,* 2019, PRRB Publishing, ISBN-1731385056.

Patrick H. Stakem, *Exploiting the Moon,* 2019, PRRB Publishing, ISBN-1091057850.

Patrick H. Stakem, *RISC-V, an Open Source Solution for Space Flight Computers,* 2019, PRRB Publishing, ISBN-1796434388.

Patrick H. Stakem, *Arm in Space*, 2019, PRRB Publishing, ISBN-9781099789137.

Patrick H. Stakem, *Extraterrestrial Life*, 2019, PRRB Publishing, ISBN-978-1072072188.

Patrick H. Stakem, *Space Command*, 2019, PRRB Publishing, ISBN-978-1693005398.

CubeRovers, A Synergy of Technologys, 2020, PRRB Publishing, ISBN-979-8651773138.

Robotic Exploration of the Icy moons of the Gas Giants. 2020, PRRB Publishing, ISBN- 979-8621431006

Hacking Cubesats, 2020, PRRB Publishing, ISBN-979-8623458964.

History & Future of Cubesats, PRRB Publishing, ISBN-979-8649179386.

Hacking Cubesats, Cybersecurity in Space, 2020, PRRB Publishing, ISBN-979-8623458964.

Powerships, Powerbarges, Floating Wind Farms: electricity when and where you need it, 2021, PRRB Publishing, ISBN-979-8716199477.

Hospital Ships, Trains, and Aircraft, 2020, PRRB Publishing, ISBN-979-8642944349.

2020/2021 Releases

CubeRovers, a Synergy of Technologys, 2020, ISBN-979-8651773138

Exploration of Lunar & Martian Lava Tubes by Cube-X, ISBN-979-8621435325.

Robotic Exploration of the Icy moons of the Gas Giants, ISBN- 979-8621431006.

History & Future of Cubesats, ISBN-978-1986536356.

Robotic Exploration of the Icy Moons of the Ice Giants, by Swarms of Cubesats, ISBN-979-8621431006.

Swarm Robotics, ISBN-979-8534505948.

Introduction to Electric Power Systems, ISBN-979-8519208727.

Centros de Control: Operaciones en Satélites del Estándar CubeSat (Spanish Edition), 2021, ISBN-979-8510113068.

Exploration of Venus, 2022, ISBN-979-8484416110.

Patrick H. Stakem, *The Search for Extraterrestial Life,* 2019, PRRB Publishing, ISBN-1072072181.

The Artemis Missions, Return to the Moon, and on to Mars, 2021, ISBN-979-8490532361.

James Webb Space Telescope. A New Era in Astronomy, 2021, ISBN-979-8773857969.

www.ingramcontent.com/pod-product-compliance
Lightning Source LLC
LaVergne TN
LVHW092344060326
832902LV00008B/798